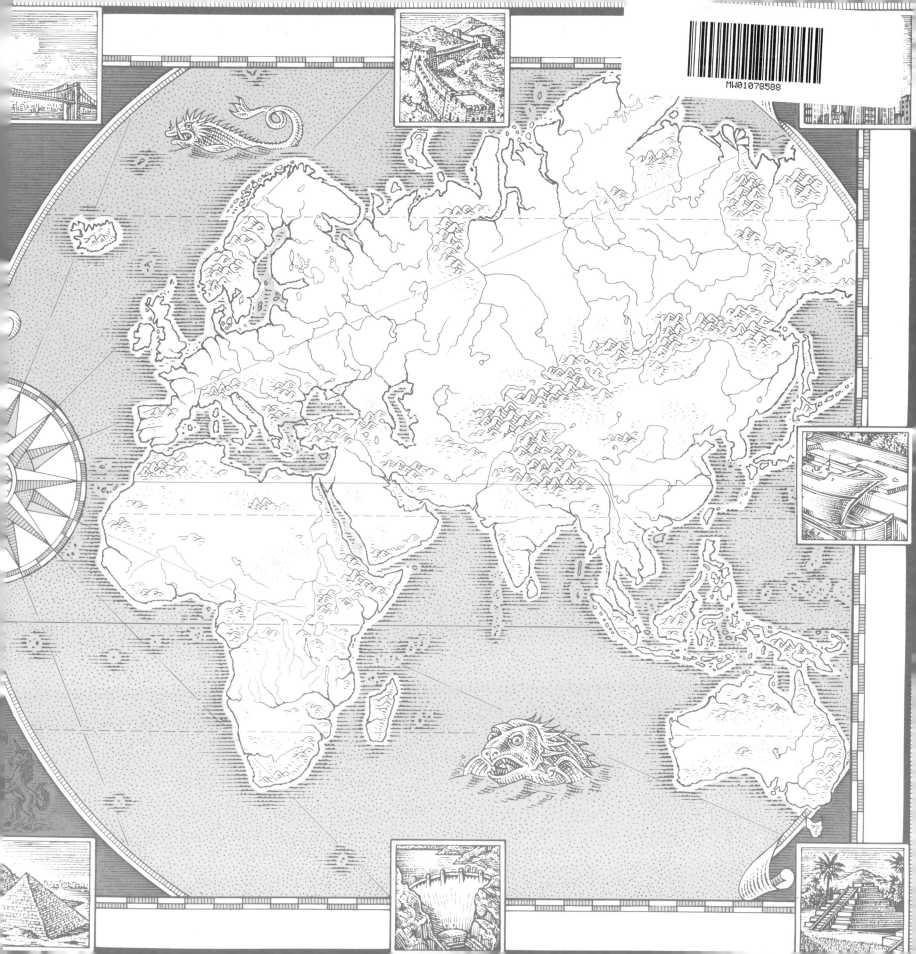

The Great Wall

MIKAYA PRESS

NEW YORK

FOR STU

*Special thanks to Arthur Waldron,
author of* The Great Wall of China: From History to Myth,
*for his invaluable assistance with the text of this book.
(Errors of fact and interpretation are mine alone.)*

*Thanks also to Professor Luo Zhewen of the Great Wall Society
in Beijing for his help and kind hospitality during my stay in China*

OTHER BOOKS BY ELIZABETH MANN

*The Brooklyn Bridge
The Great Pyramid
The Panama Canal
The Roman Colosseum
Machu Picchu*

Editor: Stuart Waldman
Design: Lesley Ehlers Design

Copyright © 1997 Mikaya Press
Original Illustrations Copyright © Alan Witschonke
All rights reserved. Published by Mikaya Press Inc.
Wonders of the World Books is a registered trademark of Mikaya Press Inc.
No part of this publication may be reproduced in whole or in part or stored in a retrieval system, or
transmitted in any form or by any means, electronic, mechanical, photocopying, recording or otherwise, without written permission
of the publisher. For information regarding permission, write to: Mikaya Press Inc., 12 Bedford Street, New York, N.Y. 10014.
Distributed in North America by: Firefly Books Ltd., 3680 Victoria Park Ave., Willowdale, Ontario, M2H3KI

Library of Congress Cataloging -in-publication Data
Mann, Elizabeth, 1948-
The Great Wall : the story of thousands of miles of earth and
stone / by Elizabeth Mann ; with illustrations by Alan Witschonke.
p.   cm.— (A wonders of the world book)
Summary : Examines the building of the Great Wall of China and the
thousands of years of conflict that preceded it.
ISBN 0-9650493-2-9
1. Great Wall of China (China)—Juvenile literature.   [1. Great
Wall of China (China)—History.   2. China—History.]
1. Witschonke, Alan 1953- ill.   ll. Title.   lll. Series.
DS793. G67M32   1997
951—dc21   97-21246
                                                          AC

10 9 8 7 6 5 4 3

Printed in Singapore

The Great Wall

A WONDERS OF THE WORLD BOOK

BY ELIZABETH MANN

WITH ILLUSTRATIONS BY ALAN WITSCHONKE

MIKAYA PRESS

NEW YORK

The battle raged around him. Horses screamed and reared. Arrows flew and men crashed to the ground. The enemy had them surrounded. The young emperor watched helplessly as his soldiers whirled about in confusion, desperately trying to protect him. He knew nothing of war. He had led his men into a hopeless battle against the Mongols. Now there was nothing he could do. Slowly, calmly, as if in a dream, he gathered his robes about him and sat down on the battleground to wait for the end.

Hours later, a victorious Mongol prince rode out onto the silent field. He was startled to find the emperor, alone, still seated on the blood-soaked ground. The bodies of his loyal guardsmen lay all about him, but he was unharmed. He did not resist as the prince led him away.

The year was 1449. Zhu Qizhen (*ju chee-jen*), sixth emperor of the powerful Ming dynasty, Son of Heaven, and ruler of all China, was kidnapped by barbarians.

The Chinese thought all nomads were barbarians. The Mongols were just one of several nomadic tribes that roamed the vast grasslands north of China called the steppe. Though these tribes had lived alongside the Chinese for thousands of years, their ways of life were different.

Very little rain falls on the steppe. There is enough to grow grass, but not enough for growing crops. Nomads relied instead on herds of sheep and horses for food and clothing. They lived in small groups, and moved whenever they needed fresh pasture and water for their animals. They lived in tents, called *gers,* and had few possessions. An entire village could easily be packed up and carried on horseback from place to place.

Horses were the key to the nomads' existence, and theirs were especially well-suited to life on the steppe. Small, fast, and tireless, they could travel long distances in the worst weather with little food and water. The nomads used their horses for hunting and fighting, and they even drank mare's milk. The horses were so prized that the nomads were able to trade them to the Chinese in exchange for grain, silk cloth, iron for weapons, and other things that they could not produce themselves.

Most nomads did not read or write, but they had no equals in horseback riding and archery. They learned these skills at a very young age, and practiced them all their lives. Small children could shoot an arrow with deadly accuracy while galloping at full speed. These skills, which made the nomads excellent hunters, also served them well in battle. They were known far and wide to be fearsome warriors.

*Most Chinese were farmers. They lived by the endlessly
repeating rhythms of planting, cultivating, and harvesting.*

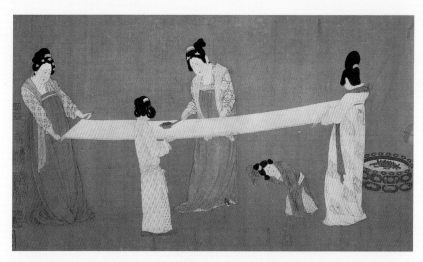

*Women wove the fibers from silkworm cocoons into soft, beautiful silk
cloth that was treasured all over the world.*

In China people stayed in one place. Generation after generation, farm families
lived in the same houses and worked the same fertile fields. They planted and
harvested and carefully stored grain for the winter months. Thanks to the happy
combination of rich soil and plentiful rainfall, China prospered and Chinese culture
flourished.

Chinese artists produced magnificent paintings, sculptures, and ceramics.
Poets and philosophers wrote important and beautiful works that have endured to this
day. Remarkable inventions, from the compass to fireworks to the wheelbarrow to
printing and paper, were developed in China.

*Scholars were respected and honored. Emperors listened carefully
to their advice in ruling the country.*

*Respectful devotion to parents, ancestors, and the emperor was an
important aspect of Chinese society. In this ritual, a son honors his father.*

The emperor was believed to be the Son of Heaven, almost a god. He not only
kept order in the society, he maintained harmony between the people and the gods.
When an emperor died one of his sons, usually the eldest, would take his place. Some
ruling families, or dynasties, stayed in power for centuries, peacefully passing the title
of emperor from generation to generation.

Order, harmony, and stability were important to the Chinese. They looked down
on the nomads and their wandering, warlike ways. They called them barbarians.

They also feared them.

The great differences between the two cultures often led to periods of conflict. When that happened, trade between the nomads and the Chinese stopped. The nomads depended on the Chinese for iron and grain, and when they couldn't get these things peacefully, they quickly turned to more violent methods.

In the autumn, when their horses were sleek and strong from summer grazing, they swept down into China, robbing and killing and terrorizing the people. Sometimes a few hungry horsemen raided a farm to steal grain. Sometimes an army of mounted archers plundered an entire city. Whether it was a few horsemen or an army, attacking nomads spread destruction and panic wherever they went. It was up to China's emperors to protect the people and restore order.

Different emperors tried different ways of defending China. Some sent soldiers to attack the nomads and drive them north into the steppe, away from Chinese farms and cities. Some tried to make peace by allowing, even encouraging, the nomads to trade with the Chinese. Others tried to keep the nomads out of China by building walls.

Walls were a defense that was as old as China itself. Since the earliest times, farmers had built them around their homes. Ancient Chinese cities were surrounded by massive walls. Hundreds of miles of walls had been built along the borders of the independent states that had existed before China was a unified country. The rulers of the independent states were often at war and used the walls to defend against each other.

City walls were many stories high and so thick that soldiers could march on the top. The walls enclosed the city in an enormous square. Roads into the city passed through tall, heavy gates in each side of the square. Soldiers guarded the gates by day and swung them closed every night.

Qin Shi Huangdi *(chin shi hwong-dee)* was the first emperor of China. In fact, he created China by conquering the independent states (known as the Warring States) and uniting them into one large country. To defend his new country against nomads, he built the first long wall.

It was a monumental accomplishment. Although no one knows for sure, it is said that Qin Shi Huangdi's wall stretched for thousands of miles across northern China. In places it was as wide and high as a city wall. According to ancient Chinese legends more than 800,000 men—soldiers, prisoners, ordinary peasants—worked for 10 years to build it. The exhausting and dangerous work killed tens of thousands of workers every year. It is said that their bodies were tossed into the earth that was used to build the wall.

Qin Shi Huangdi died in 210 B.C. and his wall was abandoned. Wind and rain gradually crumbled it into ruins. Emperors who ruled after him built their own walls wherever and whenever nomads threatened. Long walls were built and abandoned in many parts of China in the centuries following Qin Shi Huangdi's reign.

Qin Shi Huangdi, founder of the Qin (chin) *dynasty, was known as "China's first unifier." He earned a lasting reputation as a tyrant who used force to make people think as he wanted them to. This painting, done many years after his death, shows him burning books* (left) *and burying alive scholars who disagreed with him* (right).

The nomads were persistent. Even long walls couldn't stop them entirely, and raiding continued off and on for over 1,400 years after Qin Shi Huangdi's death. The raids were disastrous for the Chinese. Lives were lost and property was destroyed. Sometimes China was forced to surrender territory to the invaders.

The nomads caused great suffering, but there was never a danger that they would conquer all of China. They lived in small groups, which were separated from each other by vast expanses of steppe. Fighting and rivalry between different tribes also kept them apart. Because of their lack of unity the nomads could not form an army large enough to threaten China.

In the 13th century the situation changed dramatically. A new leader appeared on the steppe. He was Genghis Khan, son of a minor chieftain of the Mongol tribe. In battles with other nomadic tribes, he proved himself to be a talented and ambitious fighter. Impressed with his success, Mongols rode from the farthest reaches of the steppe to join him. Warriors from other tribes flocked to ride under his banner and share in the spoils of his victories.

Genghis Khan soon assembled a ferocious army and launched a far-reaching campaign of conquest that continued long after his death. All across Asia and Eastern Europe kings and princes trembled at rumors that the Mongol Hordes were approaching their borders. Cities and entire countries fell before the attacking horsemen. In a few decades, the Mongols created the largest empire the world had ever known.

Wealthy China was the most desirable prize, and it was not easily won. The Chinese fought back, but the Mongols were relentless. Cities that resisted were destroyed and the people were slaughtered. City after city surrendered. The assault continued for many years. Finally, in 1279, Genghis Khan's grandson, Khubilai Khan *(koo-bill-eye kahn)*, overthrew the last emperor of the Song *(soong)* dynasty. He took the throne for himself and his descendants, naming his new dynasty the Yuan. Never before had a Mongol reigned over all of China. China's great fear had been realized. Barbarians ruled the land.

Even the great riches of China could not satisfy the Mongols' desire for battle and conquest. Invasions of Japan and Java were attempted, and when those failed, the Mongol warlords fought amongst themselves. Efforts to expand their empire and keep peace among the warlords were expensive for the Yuan emperors. They imposed increasingly high taxes on the Chinese, causing suffering and unrest among the peasants. Rebellions began to flare up in the countryside.

Khubilai Khan was a strong and effective ruler, but the dynasty faltered after his death. His descendants engaged in succession struggles, fighting over who would take the throne. These struggles began to undermine the Yuan government. Later Yuan emperors were powerless to stop the restless outlaws and bands of angry rebels who were causing turmoil in the south of China.

A peasant farmer named Zhu Yuanzhang *(ju yuon-jong)*, knew too well the hardship caused by the demands of the Yuan emperors. His parents often went hungry during the winter months because their harvest had been taken to pay taxes.

Zhu Yuanzhang devoted himself to the downfall of the Yuan dynasty. He joined an anti-Yuan rebel group called the Red Turbans and quickly rose in their ranks to become a leader. The Red Turbans mustered an army. Gathering strength, they gained control of large areas in southern China and attracted more followers. After years of fighting, The Red Turbans overthrew the last Yuan emperor and drove the Mongols back into the steppe.

Zhu Yuanzhang hated the Mongols, but he respected their skill in battle. He trained his peasant army to fight on horseback as the Mongols did.

Zhu Yuanzhang's rise to power was quite remarkable. He was the only Chinese emperor to come from a peasant family.

In 1368, Zhu Yuanzhang proclaimed himself emperor of China and founder of the Ming dynasty. Backed by the large, well-trained army that had swept him into power, Zhu Yuanzhang ruled with a firm hand. He closely controlled every aspect of government from the Ming court to local village tax collectors, and for many years China prospered.

Zhu Yuanzhang and his son, Zhu Di *(ju dee)*, were powerful rulers, but as time went on, the Ming dynasty, like the Yuan, grew weaker. Later Ming emperors were indecisive and sometimes very young. They couldn't control the thousands of ministers and advisors in the ever-expanding Ming court, and often were controlled by them. The army became slipshod and undisciplined. The Mongols, who were gathering strength again, were quick to take advantage of the Chinese weakness.

And so it was in the year 1449 that Zhu Qizhen, Son of Heaven, sixth emperor of the Ming dynasty, and ruler of all China, found himself alone on a bloody battlefield, utterly defeated, kidnapped by a Mongol prince.

The Forbidden City, vast and beautiful, was built during the early, magnificent years of the Ming dynasty. Generations of emperors, their families, and thousands of courtiers and servants lived there in luxury, growing increasingly isolated from the rest of China.

News of the kidnapping traveled quickly back to the Forbidden City. Fear swept like a cold wind through the Ming court. The defeat revealed the shocking truth. Power had shifted. Once again, the Mongols had united and assembled a strong army. Once again, China had to defend itself against danger from the north. Court officials became obsessed with the Mongol threat. There was disagreement in the Ming government about how to deal with the enemy.

They could have chosen to attack, but the army was too weak and disorganized. It could not even guard the emperor.

They could have chosen to establish peaceful trade with the Mongols, but the Chinese were too frightened and suspicious of their ancient enemy to do that.

They turned instead to China's oldest form of defense—the wall.

The empty throne was soon filled. The Ming court placed Zhu Qizhen's brother on the throne, rather than pay the ransom that the Mongols were demanding for his return. Zhu Qizhen was eventually released and became emperor a second time.

There was no masterplan or blueprint for a Great Wall. Each emperor built when and where he thought the Mongol threat was the greatest. Construction across northern China continued for the next two centuries. The routes through mountain passes that the Mongols used most often to reach China were blocked with walls. Those walls were then connected with other sections of wall.

In the western part of the country, walls were built of pounded earth, an ancient building technique. Peasants' homes, city walls, even Qin Shi Huangdi's first long wall had been made of pounded earth. In the dry, desert terrain of western China, earth was the only building material available in great quantity. It was simple to build with pounded earth. No skilled craftsmen were needed, just many, many laborers.

Huge amounts of earth were dug by hand.

Workers carried the earth to the wall.

They piled the earth into a wooden frame until they had a layer six inches deep. Then they tamped it down with wooden pounders until it was packed solid. Another layer was dumped on top and the pounding was repeated. When a section of wall was finished, the frame was moved to the next section and the process of digging and pounding began again.

Toward the end of the Ming dynasty much building was done in the eastern mountains to protect the capital city, Peking. Builders began using bricks and blocks of stone instead of pounded earth. Walls built of stone and brick didn't erode in wind and rain. They didn't need constant repair as earth walls did.

Stone and brick walls were strong and durable, but they were more complicated to build. Progress was slow. Stone had to be dug from quarries, cut into blocks, and transported to the wall. Bricks were made from mud and then baked in kilns. Workers with special skills—stonemasons and brickmakers—were needed to handle the new materials.

Tens of thousands of workers were involved in building the Great Wall. The army provided many laborers. Soldiers became construction workers and generals became architects and engineers. Peasants were required to work on the wall. They worked for months at a time for little or no pay. Criminals served their sentences doing hard labor on the wall.

Mud bricks were dried in the sun (above) and then baked in kilns (below).

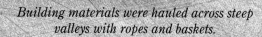

Building materials were hauled across steep valleys with ropes and baskets.

Donkeys, as well as humans, carried bricks and stone blocks through the rough, hilly terrain.

Huge slabs of stone were used as a base. Stone blocks were used to build walls on each side of the base. Earth, rocks, and rubble filled the space between the walls. The road along the top of the wall was paved with stone. Parapet walls of brick were built on both sides of the road. Drains for rainwater stuck out from both sides of the wall.

Even the most massive wall needed soldiers to patrol it. The Mongols were a determined enemy. If the wall was not guarded, they would find a way to get through. Many different kinds of fortifications were built along the wall for soldiers to live in. Some forts were large enough for 1,000 soldiers. Watchtowers, built right into the wall, were sometimes so small they barely held 12 soldiers.

The wall and the soldiers who guarded it were part of an elaborate defense system across northern China. Nearly a million soldiers patrolled the Great Wall, but they were spread thinly across thousands of miles. The Mongol warriors were outnumbered, but they had an advantage. Thanks to their swift horses, they flowed like water across the steppe. They could assemble anywhere, at any time to launch an attack and then disappear just as quickly back into the steppe. To defend against their fast-moving enemy the Chinese used an ingenious system of communication to gather soldiers together for battle.

Stone platforms, called signal towers, were built on high ground near the wall. When Mongol horsemen were spotted, a smoky fire was built on top of the nearest signal tower. The smoke was visible for miles, and when guards at the next tower saw it they built their own fire, passing the signal along. Sometimes loud cannon shots accompanied the plumes of smoke. The number of smoke plumes and cannon shots was a code indicating how many enemy riders were approaching.

The soldiers ate and slept in the watchtowers. They were ready to grab their weapons and run into battle the instant they noticed smoke on a signal tower.

The wall was shaped to fit the landscape it passed through. In flat desert areas it ran in a straight line. In hilly areas it twisted and turned like a dragon. The Chinese took advantage of the terrain to make the wall even more insurmountable. They built along the crests of tall hills and mountain peaks. The wall plunged down into rivers and then continued on the far bank. At the eastern end it ran into the sea.

By 1644, the Great Wall ran from Jiayuguan in the west, past the Gobi Desert, across the Yellow River, past Peking, all the way to Shanhaiguan on the Bohai Sea in the east. A Mongol warrior could ride for miles in its shadow without coming to a gate. And work was still being done on it.

The wall demanded great sacrifices of the Chinese people. The workers who built it were separated from their families for long periods of time. Many didn't survive the grueling work and harsh conditions.

Life was no easier for the soldiers who guarded the wall. Winters in northern China were punishingly cold and the summers were dry and hot. They were paid very little, and had to grow their own food in order to survive. Farming was difficult in the dry climate, but they had no choice.

Even though soldiers were poorly paid, the wall was very expensive. Adding to it, repairing it, and patrolling it cost more every year. To pay for it, the Ming government taxed the people of China.

Soldiers tended fields of grain and vegetables on military farms all along the Great Wall.

Gossiping and scheming, as the two men at the lower left of this painting show,
were as much a part of court life as beautiful silk robes and portrait painting.

At the same time, the cost of supporting the Ming government was increasing. Tens of thousands of people were part of the court, and more were being added all the time. Officials and advisors, well-fed and dressed in silk, spent their days quarreling and endlessly vying for the emperor's favor. Paying for the extravagance inside the Forbidden City placed another burden on Chinese taxpayers.

People grew angry at the extravagance and corruption in the Ming court, and at the taxes that were being imposed on them. Once again, peasants began to rebel against government officials. The Ming dynasty, which had been founded by a peasant, was now threatened by its own people. In 1644, an opportunity arose. A group of Chinese rebels stormed the Forbidden City and overthrew the last Ming emperor.

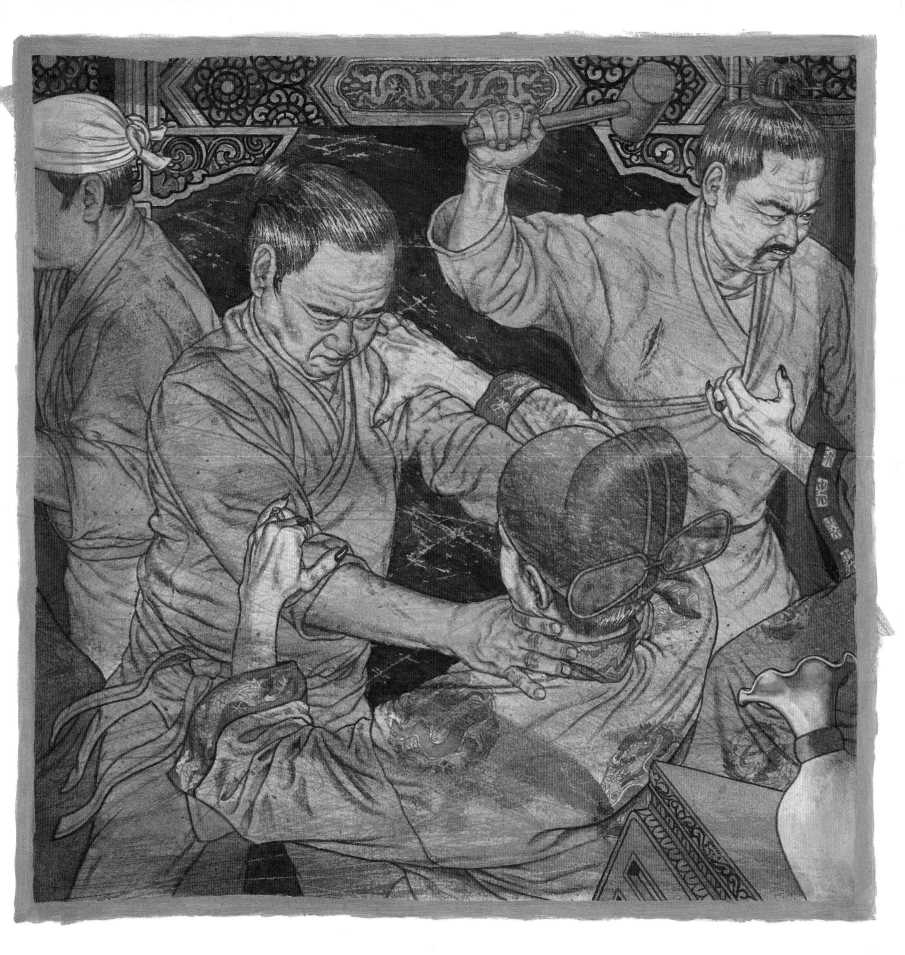

The world outside China was changing.

Once again lacking strong leadership, the Mongols were growing weaker and less united. Meanwhile, another nomadic tribe, the Manchus, had been gathering strength for years. They controlled a large area north and east of Peking and had conquered Mongol lands to the west. It was only a matter of time before they tried to expand their domain into China.

The Manchus waited. When the rebels attacked the Forbidden City, they seized the opportunity. They quickly offered to come to the rescue of the Ming dynasty.

The Ming army gratefully threw open the gates and the Manchu forces marched through the Great Wall and on into Peking. The Manchus chased the rebels out of the Forbidden City, but they did not restore power to the Ming. Instead, they seized the throne and established their own dynasty, the Qing *(ching)*.

Because the Ming dynasty had been disliked by many of its own people, it was easy for the Manchus to win Chinese support for the Qing dynasty. The combined Manchu and Chinese forces were far stronger than the Mongols. Subdued, the Mongols withdrew to distant parts of the steppe. Their fierce army, which had once so terrified the Chinese, was just a memory.

The Qing emperors ruled the land on both sides of the Great Wall. The Mongols were not a threat. The wall no longer marked a border, and it wasn't needed for defense. Construction stopped and the watchtowers were abandoned. Traders and travelers passed freely through gates that never closed.

In 1644 the Great Wall was longer, stronger, and better guarded than it had ever been before, but for the Manchus it was as though it didn't exist at all. They walked through it without a struggle and readily conquered China. The wall was meaningless.

But was it suddenly meaningless or had it been that way for a long time? Was it the wall or the Mongols own lack of unity that prevented them from conquering China again during the Ming rule? Was excluding the Mongols the best, or the only, way of preventing their raids? Would negotiating peaceful trade with them have been effective? Or even possible? We will never know. We can only imagine the fear that the Ming emperors felt when facing the Mongols, and how that fear influenced the choices they made in defending against them.

Looking at the Great Wall today we are amazed at its length, at how difficult it was to build, at the expense and effort that went into its construction. It was an extraordinary feat, and the Great Wall has emerged as the most famous and enduring creation of the Ming dynasty. We are also aware that building it severely weakened the Ming government. Ironically, the greatest accomplishment of the Ming dynasty was an important cause of its downfall.

The western end of the Great Wall in Jiayuguan. An enormous fort still guards a lonely pass through the mountains.

475 B.C.

—Warring States Period

221 B.C —Qin Dynasty

206 B.C. 210 B.C.– Qin Shi Huangdi completes first long wall

B.C.
A.D. —Han Dynasty

220 A.D.

—Three Kingdoms

265

—Jin Dynasty

420

—Northern and Southern Dynasties

581

618 —Sui Dynasty

—Tang Dynasty

907

—Five Dynasties and Ten Kingdoms

960

—Song Dynasty

1206– Genghis Khan unites Mongols

1279 1279– Khubilai Khan becomes first Mongol emperor of China

—Yuan Dynasty (Mongol)

1368 1368– Zhu Yuanzhang overthrows Yuan Dynasty

1449– Zhu Qizhen kidnapped by Mongols

—Ming Dynasty

1644 1644– Manchus march through Great Wall and conquer Peking

—Qing Dynasty (Manchu)

1912

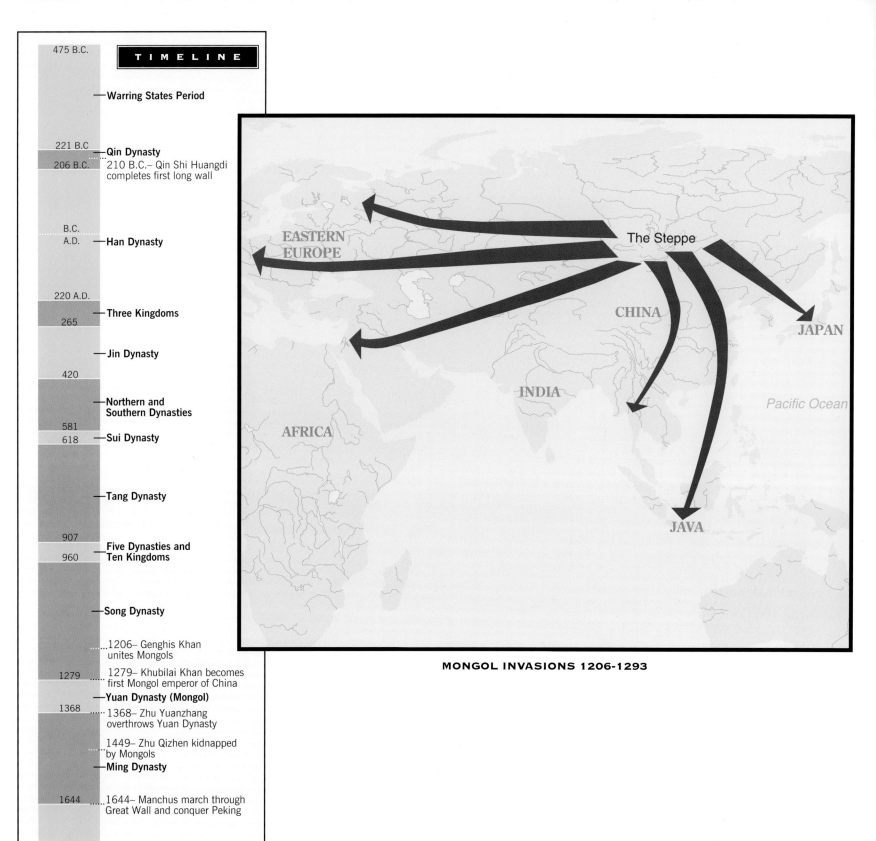

MONGOL INVASIONS 1206-1293

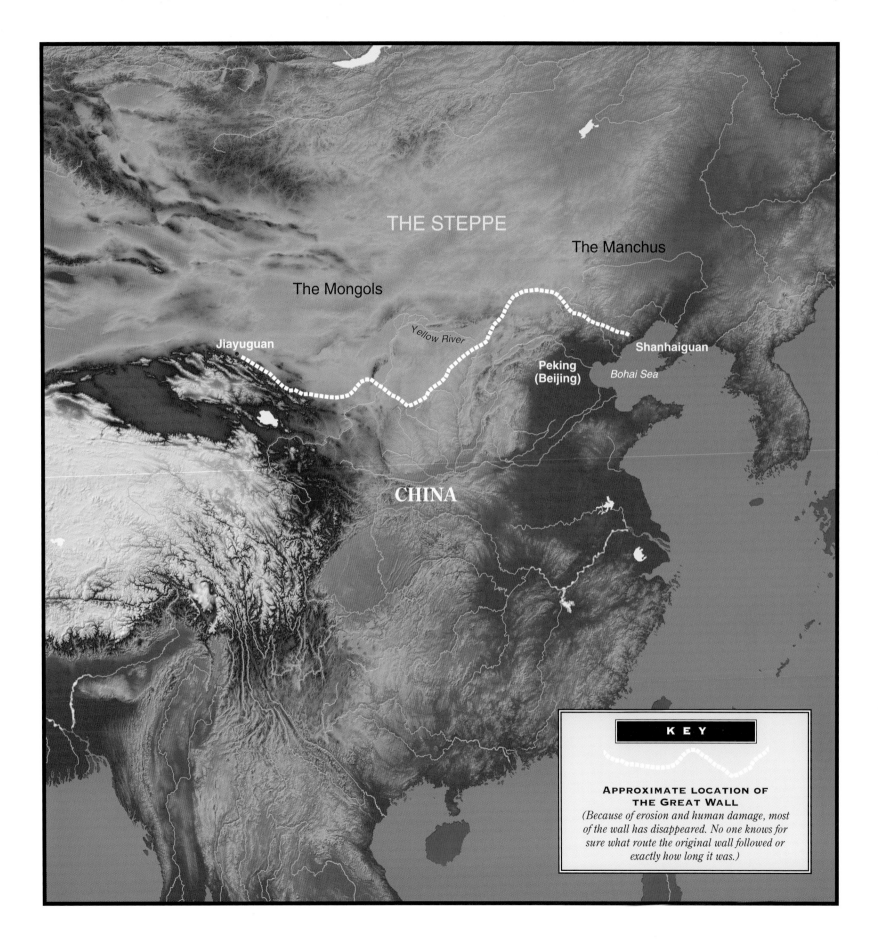

THE STEPPE

The Manchus

The Mongols

Jiayuguan

Yellow River

Peking
(Beijing)

Shanhaiguan

Bohai Sea

CHINA

KEY

**APPROXIMATE LOCATION OF
THE GREAT WALL**
*(Because of erosion and human damage, most
of the wall has disappeared. No one knows for
sure what route the original wall followed or
exactly how long it was.)*

INDEX

CREDITS

Bibliotheque Nationale, Paris/ e.t. archive: *p. 12*

e.t. archive: *p. 19*

Lesley Ehlers Design: *pp. 46-47*

Chinese and Japanese Special Fund, Museum of Fine Arts, Boston *p. 8* (right)

Denman Waldo Ross Collection, Museum of Fine Arts, Boston: *p. 9* (left)

Freer Gallery of Art/ e.t. archive: *p. 8* (left)

Wolfgang Kaehler/ Gamma Liason: *p. 45*

The National Palace Museum, Taipei, Taiwan, Republic of China: *p. 18*

The National Palace Museum, Taipei, Taiwan/ e.t. archive: *pp. 9* (right), *36*

Alan Witschonke: *pp. 4-5, 7, 11, 15, 16, 20, 23, 25, 27, 28-31, 32, 35, 35, 39, 41, 42*

0 500 1000 1500